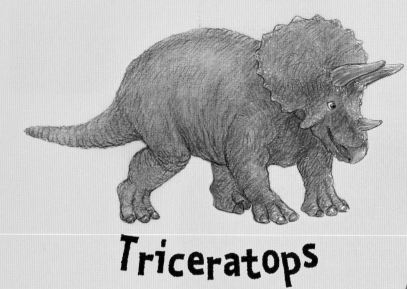

Triceratops

Allosaurus

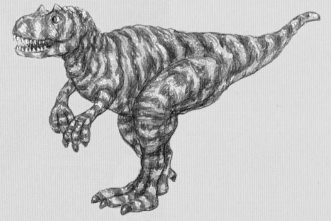

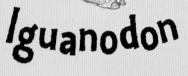

Iguanodon

Ankylosaurus

Deinonychus

Megalosaurus

Stegosaurus

Baryonyx

Styracosaurus

Tyrannosaurus rex

For Zachary

First published 2011 by Nosy Crow Ltd
The Crow's Nest, 11 The Chandlery
50 Westminster Bridge Road
London SE1 7QY
www.nosycrow.com

ISBN 978 0 85763 006 3 (HB)
ISBN 978 0 85763 014 8 (PB)

Nosy Crow and associated logos are trademark
and or registered trademarks of Nosy Crow Ltd.

A CIP catalogue record for this book is available from the British Library.

Printed in China

1 3 5 7 9 8 6 4 2

DINOSAUR DIG!

Penny Dale

One dinosaur digging,
Digging a hole.

A very big hole.

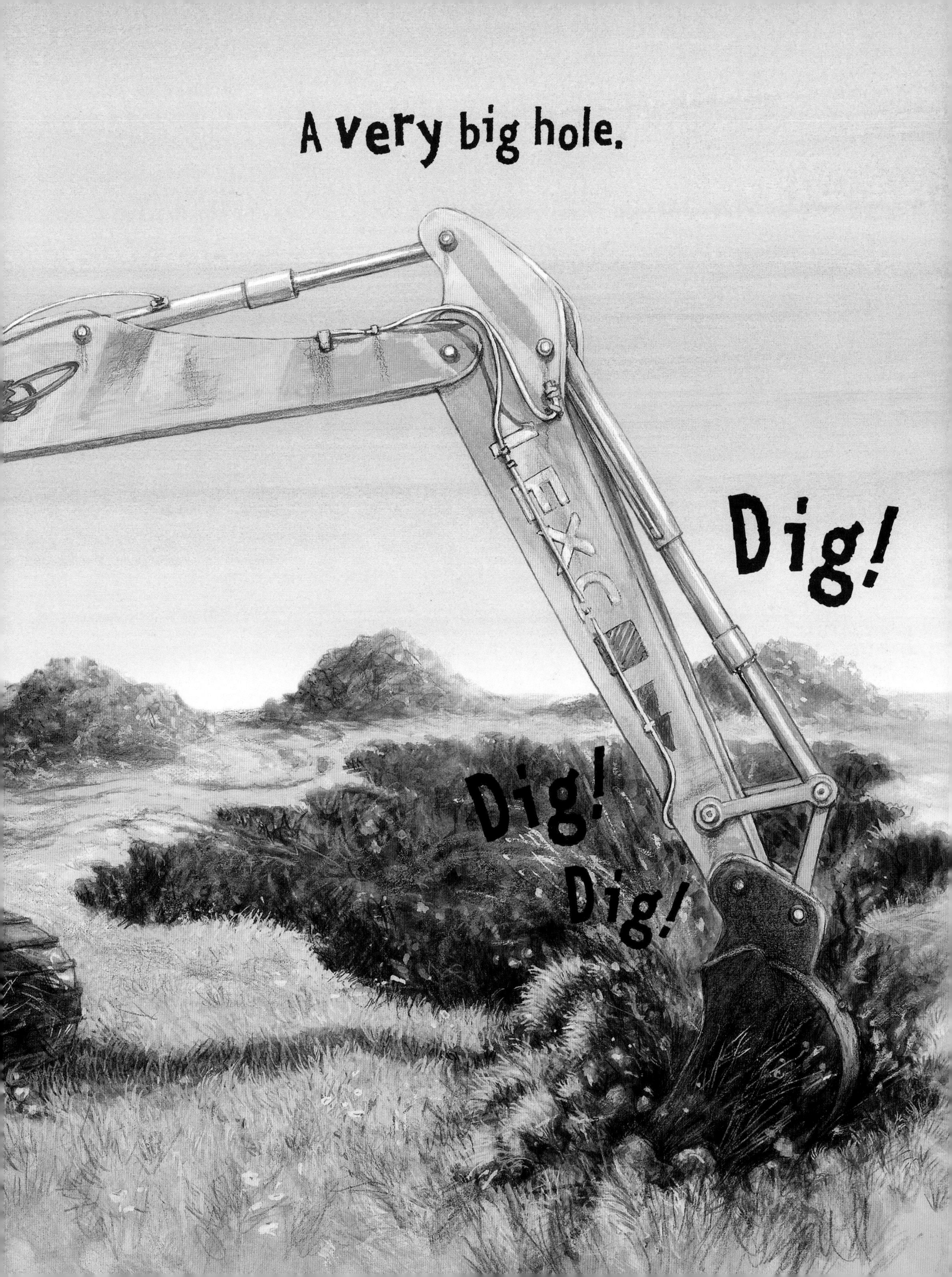

Dig!

Dig!

Dig!

Two dinosaurs shovelling,
Shovelling gravel and earth.

Tons of gravel
and earth.

Clatter!

Clatter!

Three dinosaurs tipping,
Tipping dirt and rock.

Dirt and rock,
tumbling
down.

Crash!

Crash!

Crash!

Four dinosaurs lifting,
Lifting massive blocks of stone.

Blocks of stone,
shaking the ground.

Thump!

Thump!

Thump!

Five dinosaurs mixing,
Mixing sticky cement.

Sticky cement on
shiny trowels.

Six dinosaurs building,
Building up and up.

Up and up,
into the air.

Clunk!

Clunk!

Clunk!

Seven dinosaurs **rolling,**
Rolling grit and **Sand.**
Grit and sand, flat and smooth.

Crunch!

Crunch!

Crunch!

Eight dinosaurs **pumping**,
Pumping lumpy **concrete.**
Concrete **squirts** from giant pipes.

Sploosh!

Sploosh!

Sploosh!

Nine dinosaurs spraying,
Spraying bright blue paint.

Ten dinosaurs waiting...

Watching and waiting...

Getting ready...

Getting ready to make a **BIG**...

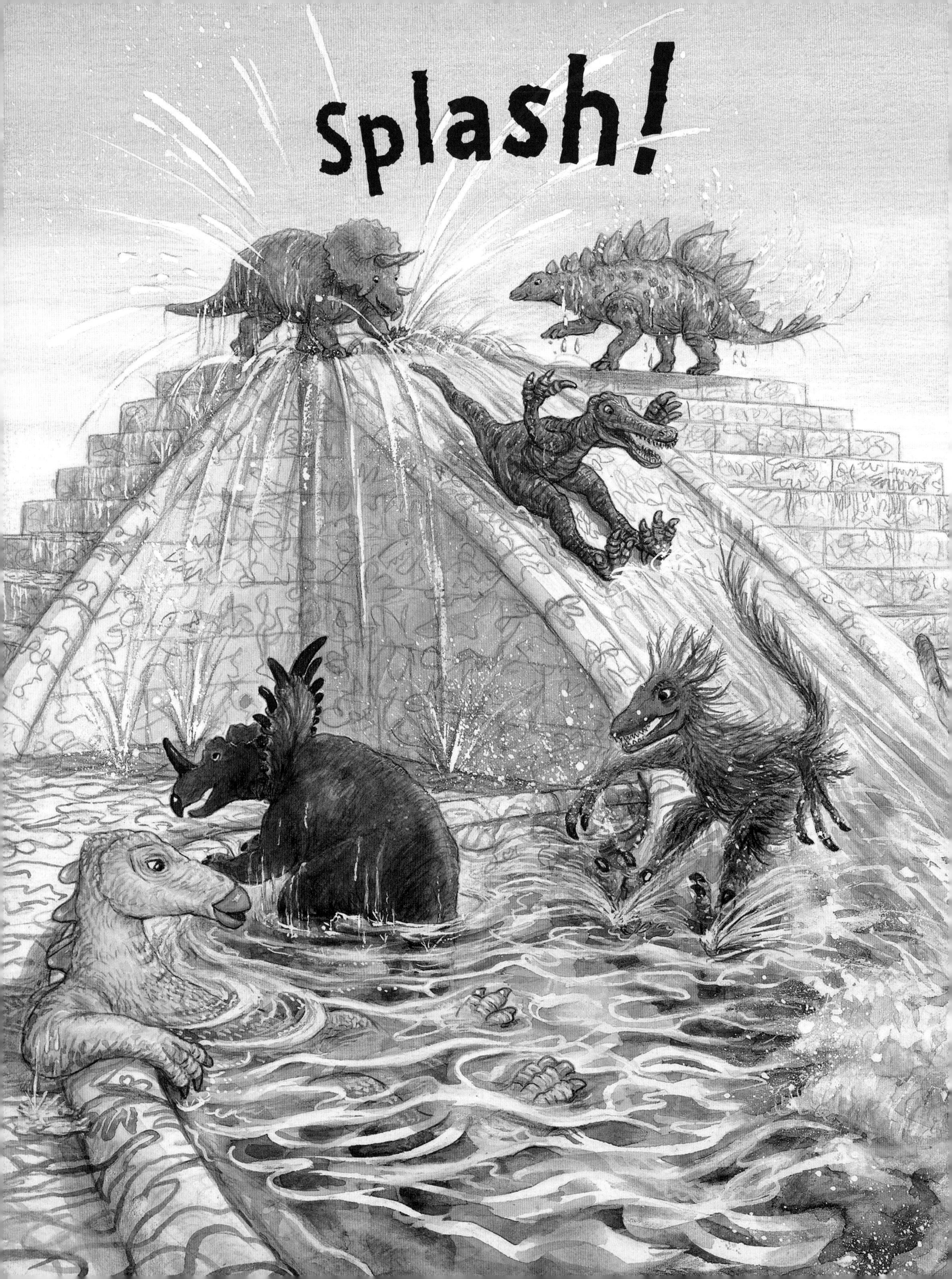
Splash!

Loader

Telehandler

Roller

Truck
Crane

Paint Truck

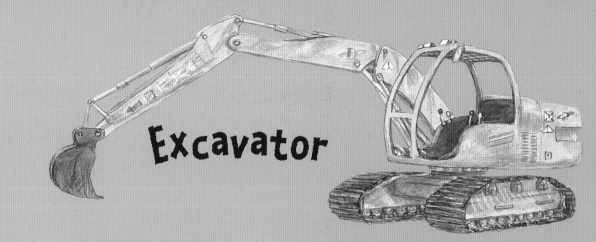

Excavator

Concrete Pumper

Truck and Mixer

Water Tanker

Dumper